Rejoicing in Hope

JAMES A. HARNISH

Rejoicing in Hope

AN ADVENT STUDY FOR ADULTS

ABINGDON PRESS / Nashville

REJOICING IN HOPE
AN ADVENT STUDY FOR ADULTS

This book is printed on acid-free paper.

Library of Congress Catalog-in-Publication Data

Harnish, James A.
Rejoicing in hope : an Advent study for adults / James A. Harnish.
p. cm.
ISBN 978-0-687-49075-2 (pbk. : alk. paper)
1. Advent—Prayers and devotions. I. Title.

BV40.H357 2007
242'.332—dc22

2007017698

07 08 09 10 11 12 13 14 15 16 — 10 9 8 7 6 5 4 3 2 1
MANUFACTURED IN THE UNITED STATES OF AMERICA

To the people and staff of
Hyde Park United Methodist Church
in Tampa, Florida,
who "irrigate the community with hope."

Contents

Introduction

When William Sloane Coffin was pastor of The Riverside Church in New York City, he described visiting Notre Dame in Paris on the first Sunday of Advent. He said the stained glass windows were "enough to lift any sagging heart." But what hooked his attention was a poster tacked to a bulletin board that contained the words of the French mystic Pierre Teilhard de Chardin: "The world will belong tomorrow to those who brought it the greatest hope."

Returning to New York, Coffin challenged his congregation to "irrigate the community with hope, because without hope, we are all literally hopeless! If we cannot feel something more, we become something less, just as if we cannot look to something above us, we will surely sink to something below us. So I'm with Teilhard de Chardin: 'The world will belong tomorrow to those who brought it the greatest hope'" (*Sermons from Riverside,* December 6, 1981; page 2).

In the same spirit, the apostle Paul challenged the urban Christians in the city of Rome to "rejoice in hope" (Romans 12:12). It was an imperative command to people whose immediate circumstances gave them little reason for either rejoicing or hope. But because of what God had done in Christ, Paul could call these early Christians to become people who would "irrigate the community with hope."

What would it look like for us to "rejoice in hope"? Eugene Peterson writes that "the Christian life is the practice of living in what God has done and is doing" (*Christ Plays in Ten Thousand Places* [Grand Rapids, Mich.: Wm. B. Eerdmans, 2005], 54). This study is an invitation to live into the stories of what God did through the lives of ordinary people who became central characters in the Christmas story, so that we can practice living in what God has done and is doing to bring hope to this world.

The questions at the conclusion of each section are designed to enable you to enter into the story and to discover the ways you can practice living in hope. I encourage you to use them either in group discussion or in personal reflection, so that these gospel stories will become your own.

These chapters emerge out of the witness of the people and staff who "irrigate the community with hope" at Hyde Park United Methodist Church in Tampa, Florida, for whom I give thanks and to whom I dedicate this study.

The Couple Who Expected the Unexpected

Scripture: Read Luke 1:5-25, 57-80.

During Advent last year, my wife and I went to see Tom Bosley and Michael Learned in the play *On Golden Pond.* The 1981 movie starring Henry Fonda, Katharine Hepburn, and Jane Fonda is one of our all-time favorites. Bosley brought just enough of his character as the jovial father in the TV series *Happy Days* to this role to be a kinder, gentler version of Norman Thayer than Henry Fonda was. Michael Learned, who played the mother in *The Waltons,* brought the same warm strength to her interpretation of Norman's wife, Ethel. The "Old Poop" and his ever-patient wife wrestle with the frustrations of aging and discover through the unexpected arrival of a child that old hurts from the past can be transformed into new hope for the future.

I left the theater imagining that Zechariah and Elizabeth might have been a lot like Norman and Ethel. Luke says they "both were getting on in years," a polite way of saying that they were as old as dirt. Unlike Ethel and Norman, Luke says Zechariah and Elizabeth "had no children, because Elizabeth was barren."

The word *barren* is as hard and cold as the ice rink in New York's Rockefeller Center. Some who share this study know how hard and cold that word can be. One of the great injustices of life (about which I intend to ask God some very direct questions when I get to heaven!) is why so many people who would make marvelous parents have such a difficult time conceiving, while so many who are obviously lousy at the job conceive like rabbits. All I can do is share the long hours of waiting, watching, hoping, and praying that link those would-be parents with Zechariah and Elizabeth.

But in the Bible, *barrenness* is more than the biological inability to conceive children. It is also a metaphor for *spiritual* barrenness.

It's the coldness of people who are unable to conceive of life the way God envisions it.

It's the emptiness of people who are unable to imagine the possibility of new life as a miraculous gift from God.

It's the sterility of people who confine all reality within the narrow limitations of our human intellect, resources, and powers.

It's the infertility of people who have no conception of the possibility that they could give birth to hope in someone else.

It's the frigidity of people who settle for this world the way it is because they cannot believe that by God's power it could be different.

Barrenness is the condition of our lives and our world when we live as if there is no listening God to hear our prayers, no life-giving God bringing new possibilities to birth, no redemptive God who might actually be at work in human history to transform the kingdoms of this earth into the kingdom of our God and to shape our lives into the likeness of Jesus Christ. Barrenness is the biblical description of a life without hope.

My guess is that there were days when Zechariah and Elizabeth's prayers felt just about as barren as Elizabeth's womb. There must have been long, dark nights when they feared that the God to whom they prayed was incapable of intersecting human experience and changing the barrenness of their lives; dismal days when they wondered if all the promises of the coming of the Messiah were more than they could ever expect to see fulfilled.

As we begin this Advent journey, some of us might confess that one of our deepest fears or frustrations in our faith life is that we sometimes feel as if all our praying, hoping, and working for a better life and a more peaceful world are nothing more than "visions of sugarplums" dancing in our heads. We make our stumbling attempts at spiritual discipline, but sometimes we're not at all sure that it makes a tangible difference. Sometimes it feels as if God has taken an extended vacation and isn't expected to return to work any time soon.

Some of us know how the poet felt when he described God as "the great absence" and "the empty silence." R. S. Thomas said that God "keeps the interstices / In our knowledge, the darkness / Between the stars." (R. S. Thomas, *Later Poems,* [London: Papermac, 1984], 23)

The season of Advent is the season of waiting for God to come. As the winter days grow shorter and the nights grow longer (in the Northern Hemisphere), Zechariah's story invites us to acknowledge our experience of the absence of God.

But then, the unexpected happened. Zechariah, who was a priest, was taking his turn serving in the Temple. He placed the incense on the altar, and its pungent aroma burned into his asthmatic old lungs. (I realize the text doesn't say he was asthmatic; but I am, and that's what incense does to me!) Suddenly, an angel of the Lord appeared and scared the living daylights out of him. Luke could hardly use stronger language: "He was terrified; and fear overwhelmed him" (1:12).

Don't skip over Zechariah's fear. We can set aside the Christmas cards with chubby little cherubs playing on puffy white clouds, or satin-gowned angels that look like Miss America with wings fluttering down from the sky. In his book *The Idea of the Holy,* Rudolf Otto used the phrase *mysterium tremendum* to describe the awe-filled dread that human beings experience in the presence of God. Every time angels show up in the gospel, the "tremendous mystery" of God's presence breaking through the narrow limitations of human existence scares the daylights out of anyone who experiences it. That's why they always have the same opening line: "Do not fear."

Gabriel announced the most unexpected news Zechariah had ever heard: "Your prayer has been heard. Your wife Elizabeth will bear you a son, and you will name him John. . . . [He will] make ready a people prepared for the Lord" (Luke 1:13, 17).

This unexpected fulfillment of a long-held hope was such a shock to Zechariah's system that it left him speechless. Luke doesn't tell us how Elizabeth felt about that; but if Zechariah was anything like Norman Thayer, it probably worked out pretty well for her. Nine months went by. The baby was born. When it came time to name the child, Zechariah got his voice back and burst into song, concluding with this powerful image: "By the tender mercy of our God, / the dawn from on high will break upon us, / to give light to those who sit in darkness and in the shadow of death, / to guide our feet into the way of peace" (Luke 1:78-79).

I'm a morning person. During Advent, the early-morning walkers and runners on Tampa's Bayshore Boulevard hit the street when the sky is dark. We get to watch the dawn break over Hillsborough Bay. In the same way, Zechariah could see the mercy of God coming like the dawn from on high.

It's a visual image of the gift of hope that goes deeper, reaches farther, and lasts longer than any of the temporary trinkets we can purchase at the mall.

Hope that God will do something in the future that fulfills God's promise in the past.

Hope that we will be saved from all the forces that contradict the saving purpose of God in our lives.

Hope that will energize us to serve God without fear.

Hope for the gift of salvation and the forgiveness of our sins.

Hope for the light of eternal life to break the dark shadow of death.

Hope for the coming of One who will guide this violence-addicted, war-torn world into the way of peace.

A spiritually searching disciple came to the wise old teacher and asked, "What can I do to experience the presence of God?" The teacher responded with a question, just the way wise teachers always do: "What can you do to make the sun rise?" The disciple gave the obvious answer, "Nothing." The teacher was silent, so the disciple pursued with another question: "Then why do you keep teaching us the spiritual disciplines of study and prayer?" "Ah," the teacher said, "that's so you will be awake when the sun rises."

Hope is a gift. We can't create it on our own any more than Zechariah could have created the child in Elizabeth's womb. We can't make it happen any more than we can make the sun rise. But we can be prepared to receive it. Our task during Advent is to train ourselves to be awake when the sun rises.

Zechariah models the ways we can prepare to receive the gift of hope. It's obvious from the content of Zechariah's song that his life was *soaked in Scripture*. The gift of hope came out of his lifelong discipline of listening for God to speak through the written word.

Zechariah's hope grew out of his lifelong discipline of *waiting in worship*. Don't miss the fact that the angel of the Lord appeared to him in the Temple. I can't promise that you will see an angel every time you gather for worship; but I can promise you that if you aren't in worship, you won't experience the angel when he comes.

The hope that came to Zechariah was *shaped in silence*. He was speechless for nine months. That's really hard for us! Our lives are cluttered with noise, from the wraparound sound in our cars to the iPods in our ears. But biblical hope is shaped within us when we practice the spiritual discipline of listening for God in silent prayer.

Evidently, when Zechariah lost his ability to speak, his other senses were sharpened, particularly his sense of sight. Zechariah could see what other people couldn't see. He could see the surprising way in which the mercy of God would break into human history. He could see the way his son, John, would prepare the way for the coming of the One who could guide us into the way of peace. He could see the unexpected hope that would soon be born. He was fully awake to see the Son rise.

Across these weeks of Advent we will discover that rejoicing in hope means that when we receive the gift, we are called to become that gift to others. Ordinary folks like every one of us are called, gifted, and empowered by the Spirit to become men and women who irrigate the world with hope.

The writer of the fourth Gospel said, "The Word became flesh and dwelt among us" (John 1:14 RSV). Theologians call it "Incarnation," which literally means "in the flesh." Zechariah and Elizabeth could see hope becoming flesh in their infant son. It was through the very real stuff of their ordinary lives that the promise was being fulfilled and hope would be made real.

Last year when our extended family gathered at our home for Thanksgiving, we ran out of bedrooms. Julia, our three-year-old granddaughter, chose to sleep on an air mattress at the foot of her grandparents' bed. Before dawn the next morning, we were awakened when she crawled into bed with us. As we cuddled together, I told her that we couldn't get up until we saw the sunlight coming in the bedroom window. Thinking that she might go back to sleep, I closed my eyes and headed in that direction myself. A moment later, Julia was tapping me on the arm. When I opened my eyes, she said, "Gampa, you can't see the sunshine with your eyes closed."

Julia was right. Zechariah and Elizabeth teach us the way to be prepared when the sun rises. Their story offers good news of great hope to everyone who walks in darkness and waits for the dawn.

Questions for Reflection and Discussion

1. Read Luke 1:5-25 aloud, with members of your group reading for each of the characters. How do you picture Zechariah and Elizabeth? When have you known people like them?

2. How have you felt spiritual barrenness? When have you faced "the absence of God"?

3. When have you been confronted by the *mysterium tremendum* described in this chapter? When have you felt fear in the presence of God?

4. Read aloud Zechariah's song, also known as "The Benedictus," in Luke 1:67-79. How does it make you feel? What visual images come into your imagination? What surprises you? Which lines speak most directly to your life?

5. Which of the spiritual disciplines from Zechariah's life (scripture, worship, silence) do you most deeply need to practice if you are going to live into what God is doing this Advent season? What practical steps can you take to practice those disciplines?

Prayer

Christ, whose glory fills the skies,
Christ, the true, the only light,
Sun of Righteousness, arise,
triumph o'er the shades of night;
Day-spring from on high, be near;
Day-star, in my heart appear.
. . . .
Visit then this soul of mine;
pierce the gloom of sin and grief;
fill me, Radiancy divine,
scatter all my unbelief;
more and more thyself display,
shining to the perfect day.
(Charles Wesley, "Christ, Whose Glory Fills the Skies," 1740

Focus for the Week

Hope is born when we learn to open our eyes to see the new possibilities God has for us.

The Girl Who Obeyed the Unseen

Scripture: Read Luke 1:25-56.

We received a unique Christmas card from a clergy friend. It was a plain, white card with these words printed on it: "Blessed are those who celebrate Christmas as a way of life."

If we take the Christmas story seriously, Christmas is not just a once-a-year event. It launches us into a new way of living that lasts our whole life long. It challenges us to practice living in what God has done and is doing in Christ. At least that's what it meant for Mary.

When Mary showed up at her cousin Elizabeth's door, the old woman cried out, "Blessed are you among women, and blessed is the fruit of your womb" (Luke 1:42). In response, Mary rejoiced in the hope that "All generations will call me blessed; / for the Mighty One has done great things for me" (1:48-49). Blessed are people like Mary. Blessed are those who celebrate Christmas as a way of life.

Two boys were walking down Fifth Avenue in New York City at Christmastime. One was headed to the synagogue. The other was going to St. Patrick's Cathedral. With some measure of kosher pride, the first boy told his friend, "You know, of course, that Jesus was a Jew." The other boy replied, "Yes, but his mother was a Catholic."

You don't have to be Roman Catholic to be fascinated with Mary. Inspired in part by the widespread interest in Dan Brown's bestseller *The Da Vinci Code* (a fun read that is about as believable as flying reindeer!), all the major news magazines have published cover stories on the role of women in the Gospels. None is more fascinating than Mary, the mother of Jesus.

Mary is often seen as an ethereal, otherworldly figure we can neither touch nor understand because she is so far removed from us. By contrast, scholars today are looking at Mary as an ordinary young woman who chose to be obedient to the Spirit of God. And that's exactly the way Luke describes her.

It's a simple story, simply told and simply beautiful! "In the sixth month the angel Gabriel was sent by God to a town in Galilee called Nazareth, to a virgin engaged to a man whose name was Joseph, of the house of David. The virgin's name was Mary" (1:26-27).

Mary was not chosen because she was the most intelligent, the most attractive, or the most religious debutante of the year. She was just like the rest of us. She didn't earn the angelic visit; she didn't ask for it; she certainly wasn't expecting it. The angel was sent by the sheer, unadulterated, surprising initiative of God.

Luke says that when Gabriel showed up with the ominous greeting, "Hail, O favored one, the Lord is with you!" (1:28 RSV), Mary had enough good sense to be "perplexed by his words" (verse 29). Perhaps she knew the Old Testament well enough to know that being "blessed" is not the same as winning the Publishers Clearing House sweepstakes. Throughout biblical history, being blessed is usually as painful as it is peaceful. Being chosen by God is usually more dangerous than it is delightful. To be blessed is to be used by God to bless the world (Genesis 12:2). If she knew her Old Testament, Mary had more than enough reasons to wonder what this all might mean.

Then Gabriel said what angels always say, "Do not be afraid" (Luke 1:30). He announced that Mary would bear a son who would be called "the Son of the Most High" God and would reign forever (verses 31-32). Mary was being invited to have a part in the fulfillment of God's saving purpose in history. It would be through the tangible, physical realities of her life that the kingdom of God would become a tangible reality in this world. And for a moment, all eternity waited to see what she would say.

Mary was a no-nonsense, down-to-earth, practical kind of girl. There's no sappy spirituality here. She sees the problem right away. Mary said to the angel, "How can this be, since I am a virgin?" (verse 34).

Mary knew that from a human point of view, none of this was remotely possible. So, the angel answered her question: "The Holy Spirit will come upon you, and the power of the Most High will overshadow you; therefore the child to be born will be holy; he will be called Son of God" (verse 35). As if to say, "If you don't believe this can happen, get a load of this!" Gabriel goes on to say, "And now, your relative Elizabeth in her old age has also conceived a son. . . . For nothing will be impossible with God" (verses 36-37).

There's no way around it: the gospel is the story of the God who makes impossible things possible by demonstrating his extraordinary power in the lives of ordinary people. It's the story of the way God intersects our human limitations with unlimited grace. When it comes to our salvation, nothing is impossible with God.

In December 1996, a water stain, sixty feet high and twenty feet wide, appeared on the plate glass windows of an office building in Clearwater, Florida. Many people believed it was the image of the Virgin Mary. They came from across the country to stand or kneel in prayer in the parking lot beside it. Hundreds of candles crowded the sidewalk beneath it. Obviously ignoring the oxymoron in the title, the city formed a "Miracle Management Task Force" to deal with the crush of unexpected visitors. When the holiday season ended, police estimated that more than 400,000 people had visited the site. The veneration continued for five years until a disturbed young adult shattered it with slingshot-propelled ball bearings.

Watching the phenomenon, I had to agree with a friend who said, "I have a near-Catholic veneration of Mary, but I can't think of one good reason that she'd want to show up on a mortgage finance office window."

A university professor in my congregation gave the scientific explanation: The moisture on the exterior of the window combined with the air conditioning blowing on the inside to cause the glass to be discolored. But as he watched people responding to it, it reminded him that there are some things in this world that science can't explain.

Back in the modern era, we assumed that the scientific method could explain everything. But in the postmodern era, people know that the scientific method cannot explain every hunger in the human soul. The widespread fascination with things like a stain on an office window demonstrates a deep spiritual hunger for things that are possible only with God. There are ways in which God works through human experience that go beyond our human capacities to explain or understand. The poet Madeleine L'Engle captured that truth in her poem "The Annunciation" in what she called "the irrational season":

> Had Mary been filled with reason
> There'd have been no room for the child.
> (*The Weather of the Heart,* page 45)

The thing that sets Mary apart is that Mary actually believed that nothing is impossible for God. She believed it so deeply that she was willing to give herself to be a part of the fulfillment of what God was doing in this world. What we have here is the story of a very ordinary girl who, in a very extraordinary way, allowed her life, her body, her whole being to be the channel through which God could make God's presence a reality in this world. And right down to this day, impossible things become possible when obedient people say yes to God and allow the power of the Most High to be at work through them.

Mary told the angel, "Here am I, the servant of the Lord; let it be with me according to your word" (Luke 1:38). J. B. Phillips translated it this way: "I belong to the Lord, body and soul, . . . let it happen as you say."

Have you ever wondered how many other girls the angel Gabriel might have visited before he found one who would say yes? This may be like some of the stuff Dan Brown invents in *The Da Vinci Code;* but knowing what I know about human nature and knowing what I know about myself, I wonder if there weren't other young women who were too preoccupied to hear Gabriel knocking at the door, too comfortable with the way things were to see the way things could be, or just too afraid to take the risk. I don't know about them, but I know about us, and I know that sometimes we miss out on what God wants to do in and through our lives because we are not willing to say yes.

I remember hearing Dr. Harrell Beck, longtime Old Testament professor at Boston University, declare with his gravelly voice that being "saved" does not mean that God cozies up to us around a campfire and croons gently in our ear, "You're saved, Mildred." It means that God looks us sternly in the eye and says, "I think I can use you for my saving purpose in this world. Are you ready, Millie?"

Mary said, "I belong to the Lord. Here I am, use me." As a result of that simple act of radical obedience, she got to sing one of the best solos in the whole drama of Scripture:

"My soul magnifies the Lord,
  and my spirit rejoices in God my Savior,
for he has looked with favor on the lowliness of his servant.
  Surely, from now on all generations will call me blessed;
for the Mighty One has done great things for me,
  and holy is his name.
His mercy is for those who fear him
  from generation to generation.
He has shown strength with his arm;
  he has scattered the proud in the thoughts of their hearts.
He has brought down the powerful from their thrones,
  and lifted up the lowly;
he has filled the hungry with good things,
  and sent the rich away empty.
He has helped his servant Israel,
  in remembrance of his mercy,
according to the promise he made to our ancestors,
  to Abraham and to his descendants forever."

(Luke 1:47-55)

"The Magnificat," as this passage is called, declares the truth about your life and mine. The proud do get lost in imagining their greatness. The rich are easily possessed by their riches. The powerful become intoxicated with their power. People whose hands are full can never receive the gift. Mary shows us that only the lowly can be lifted up; only those with empty hands can receive; only those who are hungry can be fed; only those who are empty can be filled; only those who acknowledge their weakness can experience the power of God.

Like Jesus' "beatitudes" in the Sermon on the Mount (Matthew 5:3-12), Mary's song upends the world's assumptions of strength, power, and might. It celebrates the God who brings down the high and mighty and who lifts up the poor and lowly. It defines a way of life that is radically different from the way the world ordinarily lives; a way of life that can only be called "blessed."

The Archbishop of Canterbury, Dr. Rowan Williams, sounded a lot like Mary in his 2006 Christmas sermon when he recounted his visit to the Holy Family Hospital in Bethlehem. As he cradled an abandoned newborn child in his arms, he asked the hospital director why the standard of care was so good in spite of the desperate economic conditions of the town. The director replied, "The poorest deserve the best." Archbishop Williams said, "I wonder if you can take in just how revolutionary it is. They do not deserve what's left over when the more prosperous have had their fill, or what can be patched together on a minimal budget as some sort of damage limitation. And they don't 'deserve' the best because they've worked for it and everyone agrees they've earned it. They deserve it simply because their need is what it is and because where human dignity is least obvious it's most important to make a fuss about it" (Anglican Communion News Service, acnslist@anglicancommunion.org, December 25, 2006).

All generations call Mary blessed, not because of what she had but because of what she was given and because through her obedience, the blessing was given to others. Mary shows us that the only way to be blessed is to be obedient. Christmas became her way of life from Bethlehem to Golgotha; from the cradle to the cross.

If I were to write a series of "beatitudes" based on the story of Mary, they would go something like this:

Blessed are those who live in active obedience to the way of love and peace revealed in Jesus Christ.

Blessed are those who listen to the God who looks with favor on lowly, ordinary servants and calls them to be a part of his saving work in the world.

Blessed are those who trust in the God who scatters the proud in the imagination of their hearts, who brings down the powerful from their thrones and lifts up the lowly; the God who fills the hungry with good things and sends the rich away empty.

Blessed are those who allow their lives to become a tangible, finite expression of the intangible, infinite love of God that was made flesh in Jesus Christ.

Blessed are those who allow their lives to become a blessing to others.

Blessed are those who say yes.
Blessed are those who celebrate Christmas as a way of life.

Questions for Reflection and Discussion

1. What does the word *blessed* mean to you? (You may want to look it up in a Bible dictionary.)

2. What has been your understanding of Mary? How have you pictured her? What role has she played in your life of faith?

3. How have you experienced "the God who makes impossible things possible"? When have you known or felt the presence of God in ways that go beyond rational explanation? What practical difference have those experiences made in your life?

4. Read aloud Luke 1:46-55. Compare it to the beatitudes in Matthew 5:3-12. What surprises you? How have you seen these words fulfilled? How do these words undermine the assumptions of the world around us?

5. When have you said yes to something that felt like a call from God? How did you receive that call? What difference did it make? What does it mean for you to say, "I belong to the Lord, body and soul, let it be with me as you say"?

6. How will Mary's story change the way you celebrate Christmas?

Prayer

Almighty God, who made the impossible possible through the obedience of your servant Mary, give us grace to live in active obedience to your will that we may discover the blessings that come in being a blessing to others, through the power of your Holy Spirit, Amen.

Focus for the Week

God makes impossible things possible by demonstrating his extraordinary power in the lives of ordinary people.

The Husband Who Kept the Faith

Scripture: Read Luke 2:1-7; Matthew 1:18-25; 2:1-15, 19-23.

During Advent, we are like impatient children who can't wait for Christmas morning to open our gifts. Hope is like that. Hope is the joyful expectation of something that is not yet realized. It's like the hope in C. S. Lewis's story *The Lion, the Witch, and the Wardrobe,* that one day Aslan will come to break the White Witch's power over Narnia and bring springtime. It's rejoicing in the assurance that something good is on the way. It's the hope that is sustained by faith. And that brings us to Joseph.

When he was pastor at the Fifth Avenue Presbyterian Church in New York, Bryant Kirkland preached a sermon in which he called Joseph "The Man in the Shadows." That's where we usually find him. Look at the great paintings of the Nativity. Better yet, look at the figures in the manger scene on your coffee table. The odds are that Joseph is standing in the shadows, one step outside the limelight, just beyond the candle's glow, calmly, quietly watching over Mary and the baby. He provides silent stability amid the joyful confusion and disturbing anxiety of the Christmas story. *Time* magazine finally gave him some attention in their 2005 Christmas issue, but they had to acknowledge that after a few brief mentions in the Gospels, Joseph is "severely—eventually—terminally marginalized" (*Time,* December

19, 2005; page 67). When it comes to Joseph's story, there really isn't much there.

But what *is* there is enough to give us a down-to-earth picture of a real man with real faith who struggles with what it will mean to be faithful to the promise of God. Joseph demonstrates that *faith is both righteous and merciful. It is rooted in the law, but it acts in grace.*

Matthew tells us that Joseph was a righteous man; a man who lived by the Old Testament law. That law said that when Mary turned up pregnant, she should be stoned (see Leviticus 20:10). If Joseph had been only righteous, Mary would have been dead. But instead, Matthew tells us that because Joseph was "unwilling to expose her to public disgrace," he "planned to dismiss her quietly" (1:19). Being faithful to God meant that while he respected the law, he acted in mercy. Shakespeare described it in *The Merchant of Venice* (ca. 1596–98) when he wrote:

> And earthly power doth then show likest God's
> When mercy seasons justice.

Joseph could teach us a lot about what it means to season justice with mercy. I wonder if he might have taught Jesus that lesson too.

Rumors about Mary's pregnancy were evidently still floating around Nazareth thirty years later. You can hear the unspoken accusation behind the question, "Is not this Jesus, the son of Joseph, whose father and mother we know? How can he now say, 'I have come down from heaven'?" (John 6:42).

I wonder if, about the time that Jesus was old enough to understand the gossip, Joseph may have taken him aside and said, "Son, there's something I need to tell you." And I wonder if, the day when the righteous people were ready to stone a woman who had been caught in adultery (see John 8:2-11), Jesus might have remembered that his mother could have received the same punishment. When Jesus saved that woman, I wonder if he might have been thinking of the way Joseph honored the law but acted in mercy to save his mother's life.

That's all conjecture, of course, but perhaps something of the way Joseph seasoned justice with mercy became a part of God's Word made flesh in Jesus.

Joseph also shows us that *faith is visionary. It isn't afraid to believe that improbable, even impossible things might actually come true.*

A preacher friend introduced me to a painting of the "Adoration of the Shepherds" by a fifteenth-century Italian artist named Domenico Ghirlandaio. All the typical characters are there, but there are surprises too. The artist set the scene in fifteenth-century Italy. He even inscribed the date on one of the columns that hold up the roof of the stable. Historians tell us that the faces of the shepherds are the faces of the donors who paid for the painting, with the exception of one who has the face of the artist himself, his finger pointing to the child. And then there is Joseph.

Unlike most paintings of the Nativity, Joseph commands our attention from the center of Ghirlandaio's painting, directly behind Mary and the child. Instead of looking at the child, he is looking up toward an angel who flutters in the corner. And his right hand is scratching his forehead.

Assuming that scratching your forehead meant the same thing in the fifteenth century as it means today, it feels as if Joseph is asking the angel, "What's going on here? I still don't understand it." I hope that's what the artist intended. Just because Joseph acted on his faith doesn't necessarily mean that he understood it. Just because he was faithful didn't mean that he had all the answers.

I suspect that Joseph was like Abraham, "the father of the faithful," for whom faith was not so much about having answers in his brain, as it was about the direction in which his feet were walking. The writer of the letter to the Hebrews said Abraham "obeyed when he was called to set out for a place that he was to receive as an inheritance; and he set out, not knowing where he was going. . . . because he considered him faithful who had promised" (Hebrews 11:8-11).

A few days before Christmas in 2006, Roman Catholic priest and author Richard Rohr was interviewed on National Public Radio's *Morning Edition*. Rohr said his experience of "a loving and endlessly creative God" has led him to believe in mystery. "This life journey," he said, "has led me to love mystery and not feel the need to change it or make it un-mysterious."

Rohr confessed that when he was young, he could not tolerate ambiguity. He lusted for answers and explanations. But now he realizes that "people who have really met the Holy are always humble. It's the people who don't know who usually pretend that they do.

People who've had any genuine spiritual experience . . . are utterly humbled before mystery. They are in awe before the abyss of it all, in wonder at . . . a Love, which is incomprehensible to the mind" (http://www.npr.org/templates/story/story.php?storyId=6631954&sc=emaf)

Rohr's words could be a description of Joseph. My guess is that the same questions and doubts that made him scratch his head in Bethlehem's stable went with him the rest of his life. Having experienced the Holy, he was utterly humbled by the mystery of it all and faced the skepticism of his neighbors in calm faith in the God who was beyond his human comprehension. Joseph dared to see within this impossible situation the improbable work of God. He had just enough faith to believe that this improbably conceived infant might in fact be Immanuel, God with us.

Faith isn't blind; it's visionary. It doesn't deny the improbable but hopes for the impossible. Faith keeps hope alive because it can see things that other people cannot see.

I wonder if the boy Jesus saw something of that kind of faith in Joseph. Later, when Jesus saw ordinary fishermen and called them to be fishers of people, or when he saw a tax collector and called him to be a disciple, or when he taught his disciples to pray that God's kingdom would come and God's will be done on earth as it is already fulfilled in heaven, or when he saw a dying thief on a cross and promised that he would be with him in paradise, I wonder if he might have been living out of the faith he had seen in Joseph; a faith that was not afraid to believe that improbable, even impossible things, might actually come true.

Joseph demonstrates that *faith is obedient. It takes action in obedience to God.*

Every time Joseph appears in the gospel he is facing a crisis. His story begins with the crisis over Mary's unexpected pregnancy, followed by the crisis of the forced journey to Bethlehem and the lack of room in the inn, followed by the multiple crises of the threat from King Herod and life as a refugee in Egypt. I suspect that through it all he kept reminding himself of the way the angel said, "Do not be afraid to take Mary as your wife, for the child conceived in her is from the Holy Spirit" (Matthew 1:20).

All Joseph had to go on was the hope that he, his wife, and the child would somehow become a part of God's work of salvation in human history, but somehow, that was enough.

I also discovered that Joseph never speaks. All the other actors in the Christmas drama have speaking parts.

Elizabeth, Zechariah, and Mary have songs that are nothing short of showstoppers.

The angels make the gospel sound like something from Andrew Lloyd Webber.

The shepherds talk about going to Bethlehem, and then they tell everyone what they saw.

The wise men ask the defining question of Matthew's Gospel: "Where is the child who has been born king of the Jews?" (2:2)

Like ruthless rulers in every age, Herod speaks with cunning to the wise men and with arrogance to everyone else.

But Joseph never speaks. The closest we get to hearing his voice is when Matthew records that "he named him Jesus" (1:25).

Joseph doesn't speak; Joseph acts. Almost every time Joseph is mentioned by Matthew, he is the subject of an active verb (emphasis added).

1:19: "Joseph . . . *planned* to dismiss her quietly."

1:20: "When he had *resolved* to do this, an angel of the Lord appeared to him."

1:24: "When Joseph *awoke* from sleep, he *did* as the angel of the Lord commanded him; he *took* her as his wife."

2:14: "Then Joseph *got up, took* the child and his mother by night, and *went* to Egypt."

2:21-22: "Then Joseph *got up, took* the child and his mother, and *went* to the land of Israel. . . . And after being warned in a dream, he *went* away to the district of Galilee."

2:23: "He *made* his home in a town called Nazareth."

There's not a passive verb in the script. Joseph acts. He dares to follow God's call into an utterly unpredictable future. He demonstrated the truth in William Sloane Coffin's words: "The leap of faith is not a leap of thought but of action . . . Faith is not believing without proof; it's trusting without reservation" (*Letters to a Young Doubter* [Louisville: Westminster John Knox, 2005], page 150). Joseph is like men and women in every age who are willing to act in obedience to the will and way of God with little regard for the consequences.

In the early 1970s, I had a seminary friend from Northern Ireland, where conflict and terrorism were daily facts of life. He had no idea what to expect when he returned, but he had paraphrased his own version of a prayer by David Livingston and tacked it above his desk:

> Send me anywhere, only go with me.
> Give me any burden, only sustain me.
> Break every tie except the tie that binds me to you.

That could have been Joseph's prayer as he stepped out of a predictable, orderly past into an unpredictable, potentially disorderly future. Keeping the faith meant taking action in obedience to the call of God.

And I wonder if something of Joseph's faith was present with Jesus in the wilderness of temptation when our Lord wrestled with whether he would be obedient to the call of God on his life. I wonder if Joseph's regardless-of-risk faith was with Jesus when Jesus "set his face to go to Jerusalem" (Luke 9:51). I wonder if something that Jesus saw in Joseph helped sustain him in the Garden of Gethsemane when he said, "Not my will but yours be done" (Luke 22:42). And I wonder if something of the visionary faith of Joseph was still there at the end when Jesus said, "Into your hands I commend my spirit" (Luke 23:46).

Joseph is the man in the shadows who simply does what God calls him to do, which is precisely what it means to keep the faith.

Questions for Reflection and Discussion

1. What has been your impression of Joseph? What difference has this chapter made in your understanding of his role in the Christmas story?

2. What does it mean for mercy to season justice? Can you point to times in your life when you offered mercy or received it?

3. Read Hebrews 11:1, 8-19, 39-40. How would you compare Joseph and Abraham? How do their stories inform your definition of the word *faith?* When have you taken some step of faith without knowing all of the possible consequences of that decision?

4. How do you respond to Richard Rohr's words about mystery? When have you been humbled by awe or wonder? How do you deal with doubts or questions about your faith?

5. What current steps of obedience is God calling you to take?

6. How does the story of Joseph have an impact upon your understanding of what it means to "keep the faith"? How is faith related to hope?

Prayer

O God, who from the family of your servant David raised up Joseph to be the guardian of your incarnate Son and the spouse of his virgin mother: Give us grace to imitate his uprightness of life and his obedience to your commands; through Jesus Christ our Lord, who lives and reigns with you and the Holy Spirit, one God, for ever and ever. Amen. (*The Book of Common Prayer,* page 239)

Focus for the Week

Hope is born through faith that is grace-filled, visionary, and obedient.

Fourth Week of Advent

The Witnesses Who Confirmed the Hope

Scripture: Read Luke 2:21-38.

Moorhead Kennedy was the United States Foreign Secretary in Iran in 1979 when he became one of the hostages who spent 444 days in captivity. None of us who lived through that time will forget the unlighted Christmas tree on the White House grounds that year. After his return, Kennedy became the director of the Cathedral Peace Institute at the Cathedral of St. John the Divine in New York. Looking back on his captivity, he wrote, "In the end, we hostages learned how to live on hope . . . When hope becomes credible, extremists lose their credibility" (*The Ayatollah in the Cathedral: Reflections of a Hostage,* pages 163, 209).

How does hope become credible? What evidence do we need to keep hoping when hope seems hopeless? What keeps hope alive over the long haul?

I've never seen a Christmas card that featured Simeon and Anna. None of the carols contain Simeon's song, the *Nunc dimittis.* Simeon and Anna are the easily forgotten, often-ignored characters in Luke's version of the birth narrative. They come onstage, so to speak, after the tree has been taken down, the decorations packed away, and the candle wax cleaned off the church carpet. But for Luke, the birth story would be incomplete without them.

Simeon was old enough to play "Father Time" on New Year's Eve. If you had been a regular worshiper in the Temple, you would have recognized him. He was there every time they opened the doors. Everyone said he was a "righteous" man.

I imagine that the older he got, the more devout he became. I suspect he sat in the corner, reading the prophets, Isaiah mostly, with the promises of One who would bring the rule and reign of God into human history. The old man loved the ancient promises, but when you looked into his eyes, you sensed that his inner compass was set on something that was yet to come: it was the promise that he would not die until he had seen the Messiah.

Anna was old too, eighty-four, to be exact. She spent most of her time in worship, often in fasting and prayer. None of the other Gospels mentions these two old folks, but I love them. I've known people like them in every church I've served. Folks whose bodies are old in years, but whose spirits are young in hope; people who love the past, but whose hearts are set on the future.

Finally, the day came for which both of them had been waiting. Simeon noticed an ordinary couple who brought their forty-day-old baby boy to the Temple to dedicate him to the Lord. They gave the offering of a pair of turtledoves or two pigeons, the legal option for families who were too poor to afford a lamb.

Simeon probably couldn't explain it. There are some things you just know because you know. He took the baby in his bony old hands and lifted him as high as his arthritic old arms would let him. Then he prayed, "Lord, let your servant depart in peace, for I have seen the Lord's salvation" (from Luke 2:29-30). That's when Anna came in. When she saw the baby, she praised God and ran off to tell everyone else about it.

It's a beautiful story beautifully told. Luke's primary purpose is theological. He uses Simeon and Anna to establish the identity of Jesus. These two old saints who represent the long history of hope from the past become the witnesses to what God is doing in the present and what God will do in the future.

Simeon and Anna teach us that *hope becomes credible when it is defined by Jesus.* Right at the beginning, Luke wants us to know that the singular sign of God's salvation is the life, death, and resurrection of Jesus. God's Word did not become more words, it became flesh. In the words, will, and way of Jesus, we see God's saving work in human experience. He is the sign by which our lives and world will rise or fall.

Eugene Peterson writes that "Jesus is the name that keeps us attentive to the God-defined, God-revealed life. The amorphous limpness so often associated with 'spirituality' is given skeleton, sinews, definition, shape and energy by the term 'Jesus.' Jesus is the central and defining figure in the spiritual life" (*Christ Plays in Ten Thousand Places,* page 31).

What matters most for Simeon, for Luke, and for everyone who enters into the gospel story is simply getting to know Jesus. Hope becomes credible when it is consistent with him.

But for Luke, this event also tells us something about Mary. Phillip Yancey writes that "often a work of God comes with two edges, great joy and great pain, and . . . Mary embraced both" (*The Jesus I Never Knew,* page 32). Along with the prediction that Mary's child would be a light for the Gentiles and glory for Israel, Simeon warned Mary, "A sword will pierce your own soul too" (Luke 2:35).

Simeon's words teach us that *hope becomes credible when it takes in both joy and pain.* It's the truth we'd like to avoid at Christmas. We prefer the virgin Mary cradling the baby in the manger over the mature Mary of Michelangelo's *Pietà,* cradling the lifeless body of Jesus in her arms. Yancey writes, "We observe a mellow, domesticated holiday purged of . . . any reminder of how the story that began at Bethlehem turned out at Calvary" (*The Jesus I Never Knew,* page 33). Luke uses Simeon's song to link them together: Bethlehem and Golgotha, joy and pain, hope and fear, life and death, just the way Phillips Brooks taught us to sing on Christmas Eve, "The hopes and fears of all the years are met in thee tonight" ("O Little Town of Bethlehem," 1868).

After a quarter of a century of pastoral experience in South Africa, much of it during the difficult struggle against apartheid, Trevor Hudson says, "My experience with my suffering neighbor is where I meet the crucified and risen Christ" (*A Mile in My Shoes,* page 41). In his book, Hudson describes his plan for "A Pilgrimage of Pain and Hope" that enables others to experience the hope that takes in both joy and pain.

Simeon also shows us that *hope becomes credible when it sees the future in the present.* I love the way Simeon says, "I can die in peace because I have seen the Lord's salvation," but, of course, he did not live long enough to see that salvation fulfilled.

He wasn't among the teachers the adolescent Jesus questioned in the Temple (see Luke 2:41-52).

He didn't witness Jesus' baptism when the dove descended and a voice from heaven declared, "You are my Son, the Beloved" (Luke 3:21-22).

He wasn't in the synagogue when Jesus announced his Kingdom agenda with the words of Isaiah (see Luke 4:14-21).

He never saw people healed and demons cast out (see Luke 4:31-44).

He never heard Jesus' description of life in the kingdom of God (see Luke 6:17-49).

He didn't shout "Hosanna!" with the Palm Sunday throngs (see Luke 19:28-38).

He didn't watch Jesus die on the cross (see Luke 23:26-49).

He never met the risen Christ on the road to Emmaus (see Luke 24:13-35).

And he wasn't in the upper room to experience the coming of the Holy Spirit (see Acts 2:1-21).

Simeon never saw the fulfillment of God's salvation in the life, death, and resurrection of Jesus; but it was enough for him to have been there to see this child. He could rejoice in the hope of the salvation that would be fulfilled in Jesus. He could see what God would do in the future because of what God had shown him in the present.

Hope is like that. Hope doesn't need to have all the answers or see all the results. In fact, Paul tells the Romans that "hope that is seen is not hope." But in the same breath, he assures them that "in hope we were saved" (Romans 8:24-25).

During the season of Advent, faithful disciples learn to look in two directions at the same time. We look back to that moment in history when Christ came among us as a child in the manger, and we look forward to the conclusion of history when Christ will come as the fulfillment of God's kingdom coming on earth as it is in heaven. Simeon bears witness to the hope of people who, even when their world seems to be falling apart around them, can see the Spirit of God at work to bring new life and new creation. We've seen that hope in Jesus.

An interviewer once asked Billy Graham if he was an optimist or a pessimist. Dr. Graham said he was an optimist. The interviewer asked how he could be an optimist in a world like this. Dr. Graham said that he had read the last page of the New Testament and he knows how the story comes out in the end. That's hope.

Some folks have made this Advent journey feeling as if the realities upon which we've depended in the past are crumbling around us. Some have faced tremendous loss since last Christmas. Some come to this Christmas with dashed hopes and broken dreams. Some look to the year ahead with anxiety and fear. The good news of hope for each of us is that we have seen the credible sign of God's hope in the birth, life, death, and resurrection of Jesus. Like Simeon and Anna, we may not see all the promises of the Kingdom fulfilled, but we have seen enough to live into what God has done and is doing. Along the way to the fulfillment of the promise, we can rejoice in hope!

Questions for Reflection and Discussion

1. How do you picture Simeon and Anna? Who have you known who might be like them?

2. How do you define *hope*? How have you experienced it? What difference does it make to define hope by the life, death, and resurrection of Jesus? What's the difference between hope and optimism?

3. What difference does it make for you to connect Bethlehem with Calvary? How have you known hope that contains both joy and pain? When have you experienced the presence of the risen Christ in suffering? (You may want to follow this study with Trevor Hudson's book *A Mile in My Shoes*, published by Upper Room Books.)

4. How can you identify with Simeon's hope? What signs of God's work in the past and present give you hope for what God will do in the future? How does that hope shape the way you live today?

5. What new discoveries have you made during this Advent journey? How will these discoveries change your Christmas celebration? What difference will Christmas make in the way you live in the year ahead?

Prayer

O holy Child of Bethlehem, descend to us, we pray;
Cast out our sin, and enter in, be born in us today.
We hear the Christmas angels the great glad tidings tell;
O come to us, abide with us, our Lord Emmanuel!
("O Little Town of Bethlehem, Phillips Brooks, 1868)

Focus for the Week

Hope becomes credible in the life, death, and resurrection of Jesus.